HOW TO USE THE COMPASS

Imagine the compass as a little helper that always points toward the Earth's North. Hold the book flat and the needle will spin until the red arrow stops. Turn the book so the red arrow lines up with the **N**. This is North. Once you know where North is, it's easy to find the other directions: South is the opposite of North, East is to the right of North, and West is to the left of North.

To follow the epic animal journeys, look out for the directions that appear next to the compass on each page.

Wildebeest, East Africa

Simply turn the book until the compass needle is pointing in the right direction, and you are looking in the direction of the animals on their amazing journeys!

This works the same way whether you're in the northern or southern half of the world—North is always North, and your compass will show you the direction the animals are traveling every time!

SNOW, ICE—AND WOLVES!

In northern North America lives a type of deer called caribou. Each spring, as the ice and snow melt, the caribou set off to travel even farther north, to the windy, hilly plains of the high Arctic. Here the young are born and the herds have plenty of food—and there are fewer wolves and other predators. In the fall, they return south again, where it is still icy and snowy but less cold.

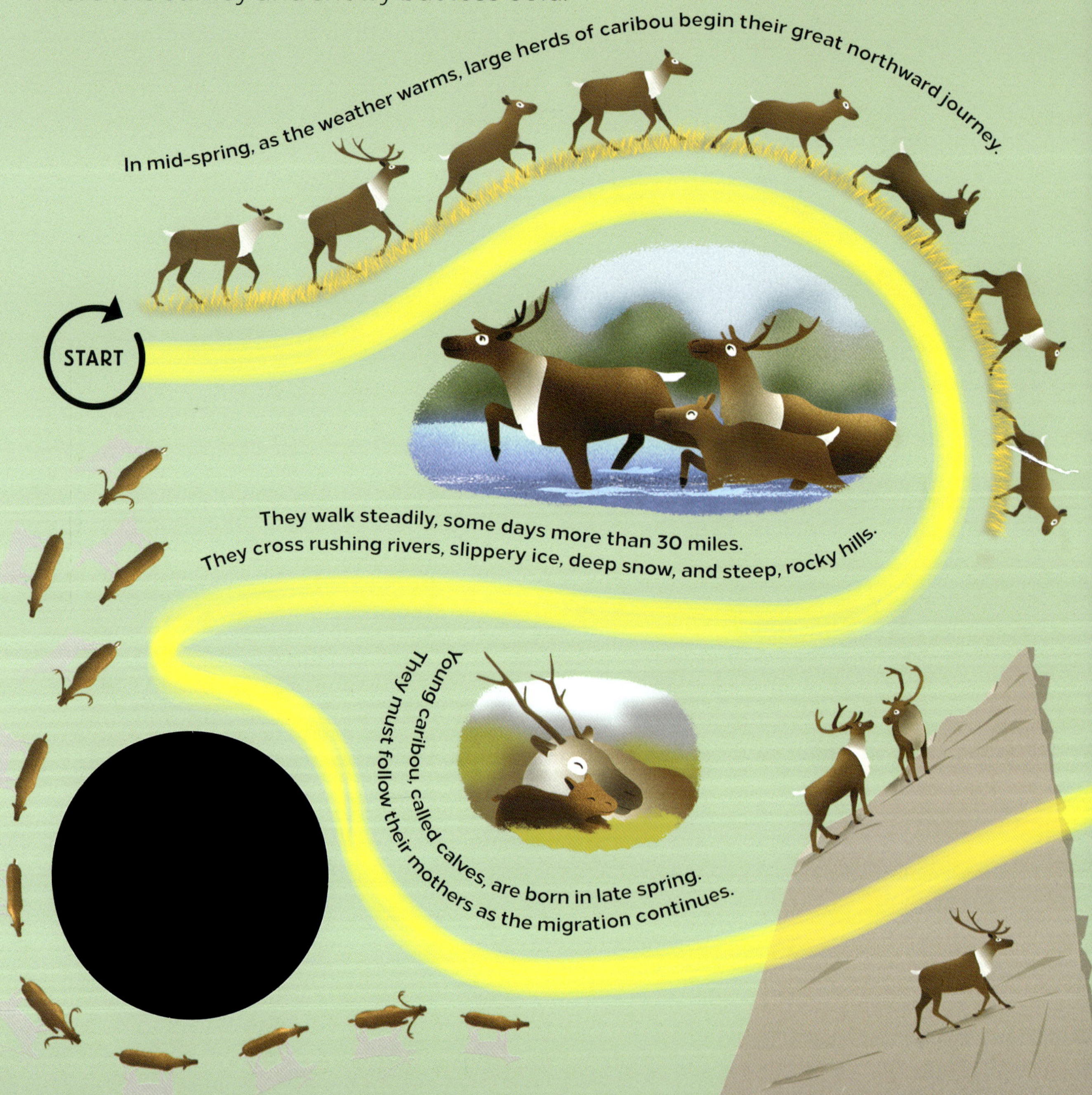

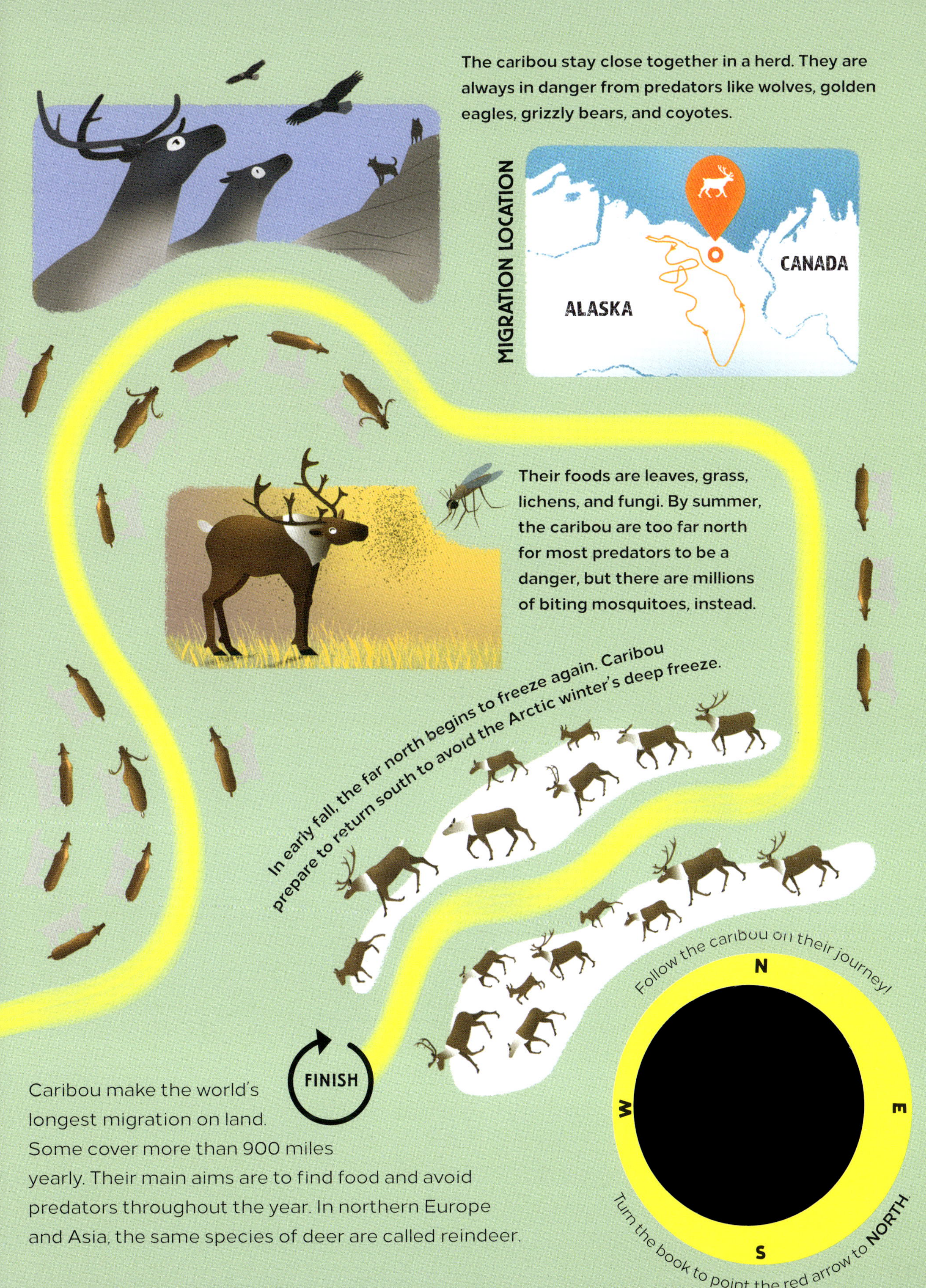

The caribou stay close together in a herd. They are always in danger from predators like wolves, golden eagles, grizzly bears, and coyotes.

Their foods are leaves, grass, lichens, and fungi. By summer, the caribou are too far north for most predators to be a danger, but there are millions of biting mosquitoes, instead.

In early fall, the far north begins to freeze again. Caribou prepare to return south to avoid the Arctic winter's deep freeze.

Caribou make the world's longest migration on land. Some cover more than 900 miles yearly. Their main aims are to find food and avoid predators throughout the year. In northern Europe and Asia, the same species of deer are called reindeer.

THE GREAT MIGRATION

Many migrating animals make a journey in a single direction, then come back along the same route. In East Africa, more than one million wildebeest follow a huge circular migration, some covering more than 600 miles. Some of the vast herds are 24 miles long! There is no real beginning or end—the great wildebeest migration continues year after year following the rains needed for the wildebeests' plant food to grow.

The wildebeest travel north, swimming across the wide Mara River, which teems with hungry crocodiles. Lions, leopards, and hyenas are constant dangers.

When the dry season arrives in the Serengeti, food soon becomes scarce. The wildebeest begin their journey back to the Maasai Mara, following fresh food and water on the way. Thousands of zebras and giraffes join the migration for a time, then move on.

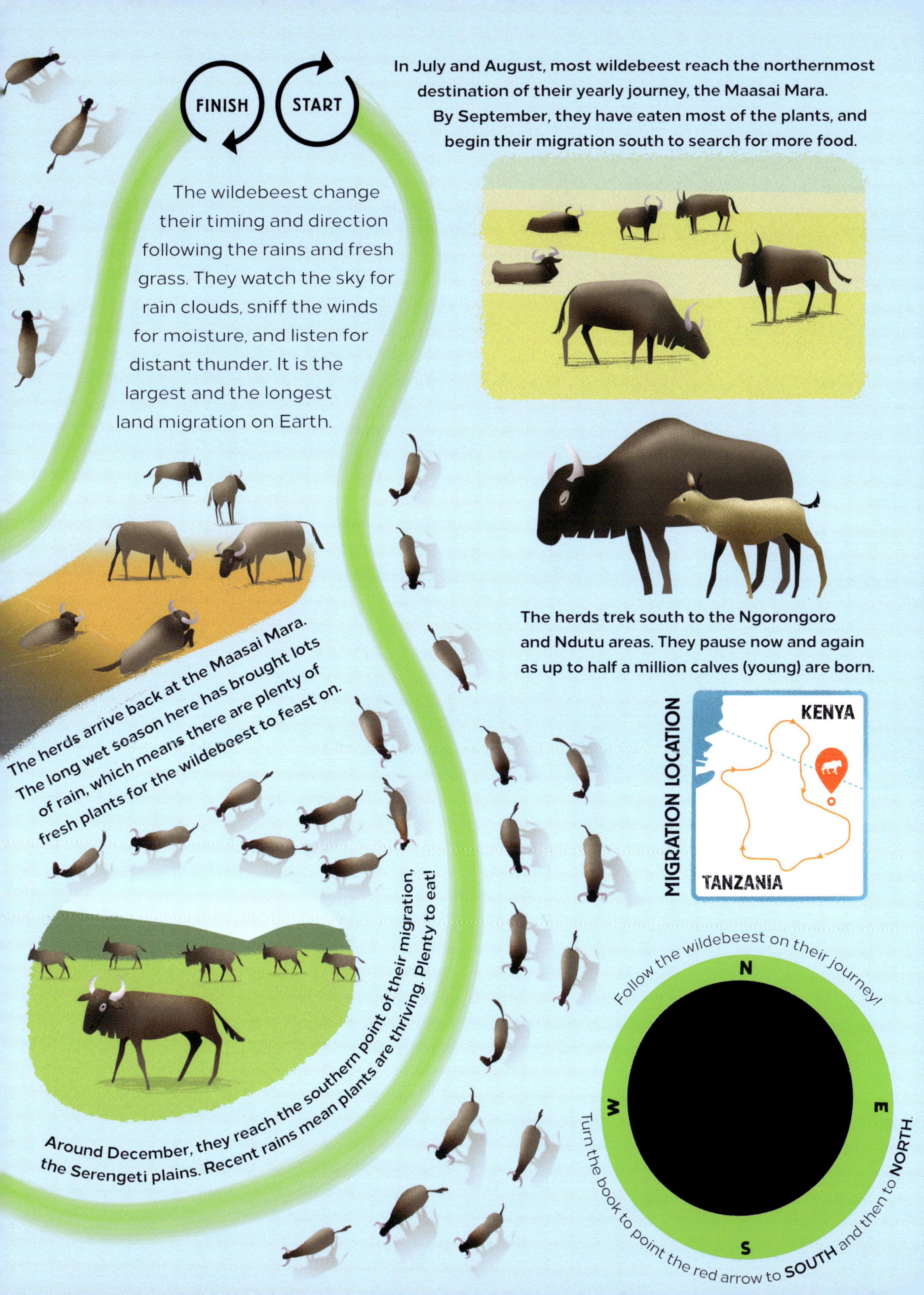
FINISH
START
In July and August, most wildebeest reach the northernmost destination of their yearly journey, the Maasai Mara. By September, they have eaten most of the plants, and begin their migration south to search for more food.
The wildebeest change their timing and direction following the rains and fresh grass. They watch the sky for rain clouds, sniff the winds for moisture, and listen for distant thunder. It is the largest and the longest land migration on Earth.
The herds trek south to the Ngorongoro and Ndutu areas. They pause now and again as up to half a million calves (young) are born.
The herds arrive back at the Maasai Mara. The long wet season here has brought lots of rain, which means there are plenty of fresh plants for the wildebeest to feast on.
MIGRATION LOCATION
KENYA
TANZANIA
Around December, they reach the southern point of their migration, the Serengeti plains. Recent rains mean plants are thriving. Plenty to eat!
Follow the wildebeest on their journey!
N
E
S
W
Turn the book to point the red arrow to SOUTH and then to NORTH.

GATHERING OF THE GIANTS

Elephants are the biggest land animals. They have enormous appetites, so they are often on the move to find fresh food. About 6,000 wild Asian elephants live on the island of Sri Lanka. During its dry season, mainly July to September, hundreds of elephants from all over the island's northern regions migrate south to one place, Minneriya National Park. Here, there are plenty of grasses, leaves, and other plants to eat, and new friends to make, too.

The dry season starts in June or July. Food becomes scarce. From all around the region, elephants travel to the same place—Minneriya

For most of the year, Sri Lanka's wild elephants roam around their local forests, grasslands, and bush. They usually travel only a few miles a day searching for food.

All the elephants in the region know there is food and water at Minneriya, even in the driest times. People gather, too. They watch as the elephants relax, feed, bathe, and "talk" by making many different sounds and stroking each other with their trunks.

Minneriya has a huge lake with wide shores. In the dry season falling water levels reveal damp, muddy grasslands.

The lake is not a natural lake. People made it 1,700 years ago. They built a river dam with walls around it. Water collected as an enormous storage reservoir or "tank."

The elephants love the muddy pools and lush grass. They mingle together, meet old friends, and make new ones. The young play together.

As the rainy season begins, most elephants return to their homes in the north, some more than 50 miles away. About 100 elephants stay at Minneriya all year.

BEARDS AND TROTTERS

The bearded pigs of Southeast Asia really have beards of long hair on their cheeks and chins! They also complete amazing migrations. For most of the year, bearded pigs stay in forests, females with their young, and males on their own. But at certain times they gather in herds of many hundreds to migrate, sometimes for more than 60 miles. The pigs head for areas where there are fresh fruits, shoots, and other food to eat. Bearded pigs eat almost anything!

Bearded pigs are the only pigs that migrate, but habitat loss threatens the future of this journey. Forest trees are cut down for timber and crops are planted. The pigs need to eat so they raid the crops. But people chase them away or kill them for their meat. Much work needs to be done to secure their future.

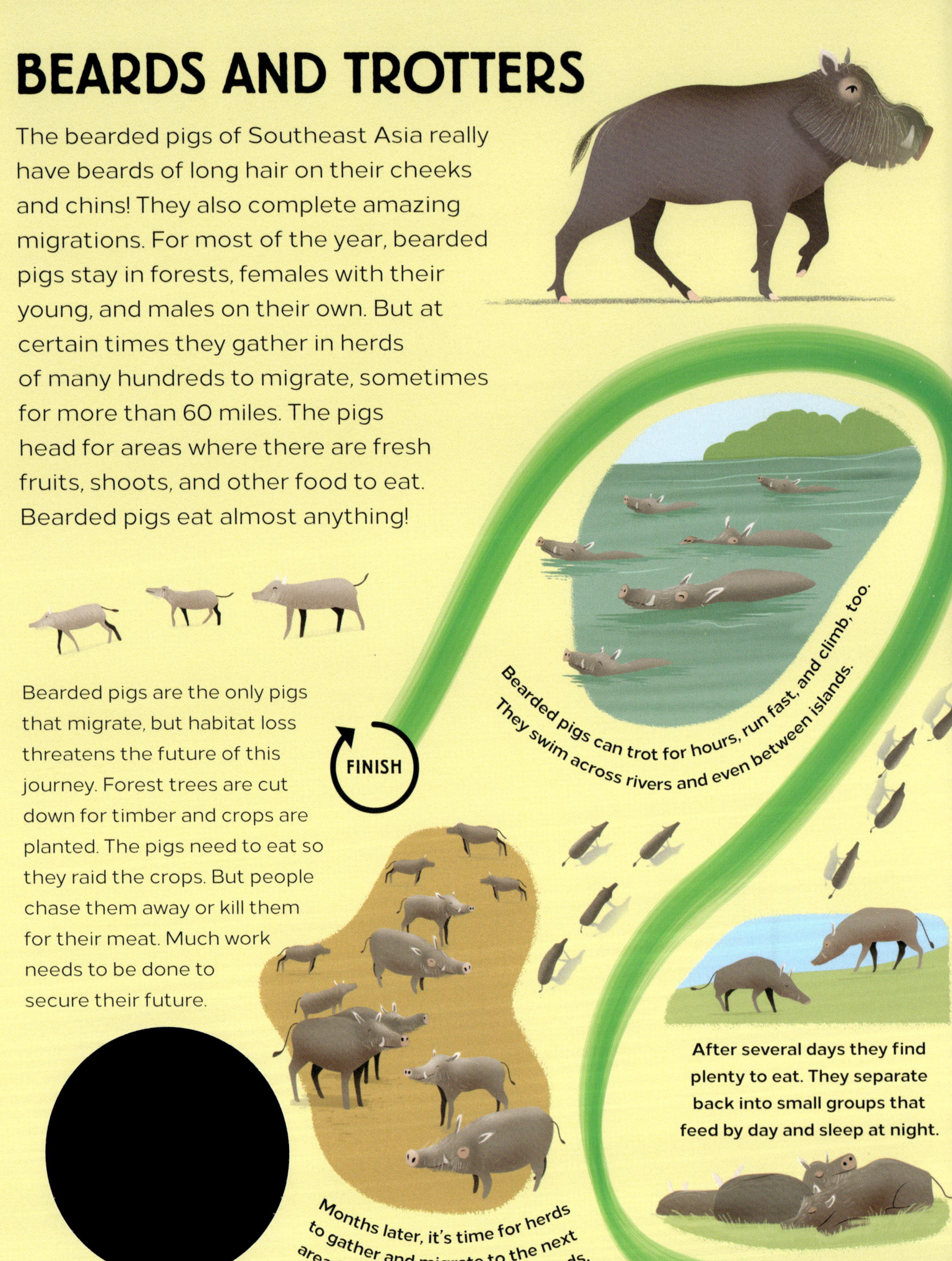

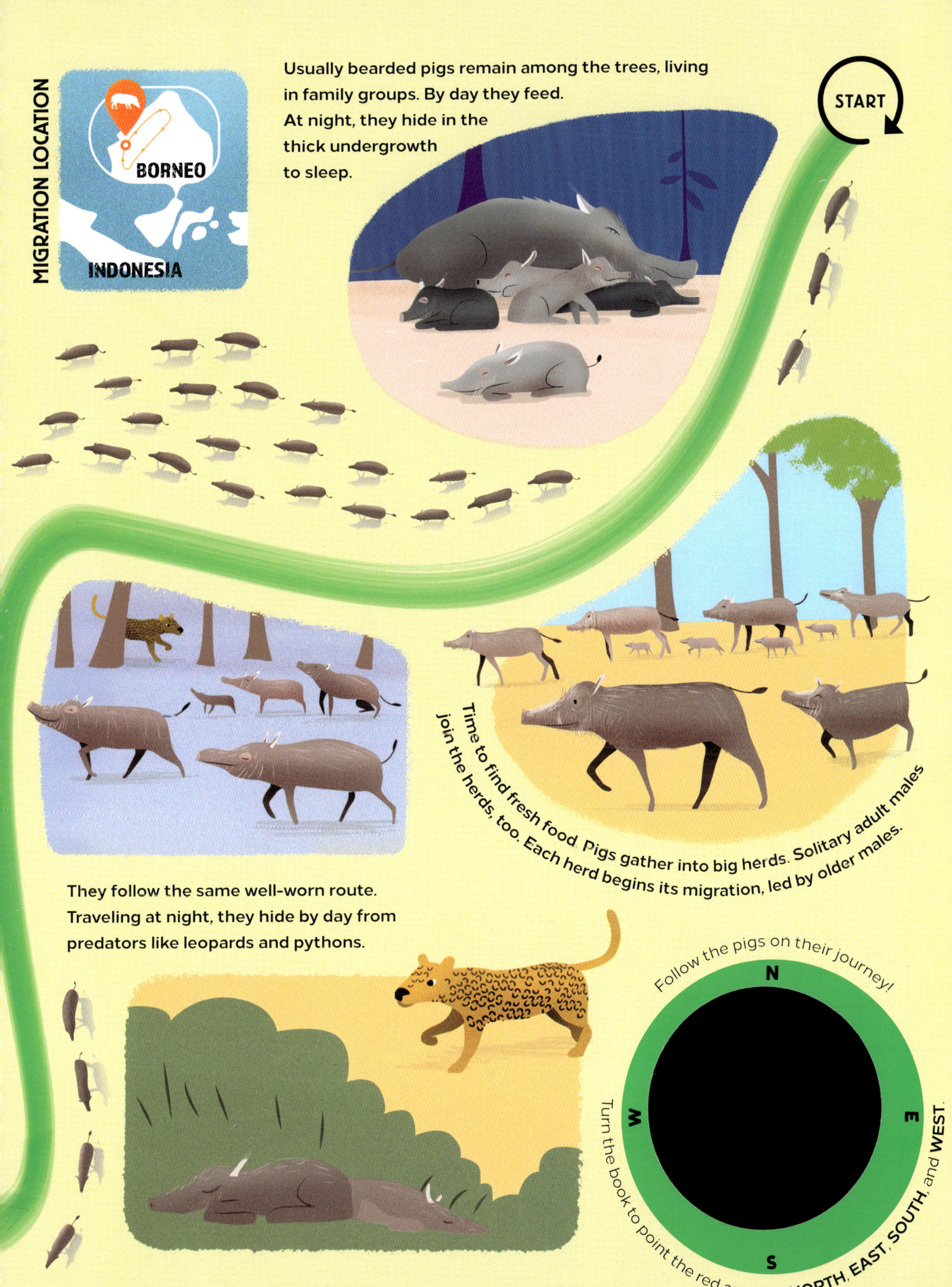
MIGRATION LOCATION
BORNEO
INDONESIA
START
Usually bearded pigs remain among the trees, living in family groups. By day they feed. At night, they hide in the thick undergrowth to sleep.
Time to find fresh food. Pigs gather into big herds. Solitary adult males join the herds, too. Each herd begins its migration, led by older males.
They follow the same well-worn route. Traveling at night, they hide by day from predators like leopards and pythons.
Follow the pigs on their journey!
N
E
S
W
Turn the book to point the red arrow to NORTH, EAST, SOUTH, and WEST.

UP AND DOWN THE ANDES

Guanacos are members of the camel family, and wild relatives of llamas and alpacas. There are up to two million guanacos in South America. Most stay in the same area all year, but a few thousand guanacos make a migration up and down the mountains. In spring, guanacos migrate up to the highlands to graze on summer grasses, shrubs, and flowers. As winter arrives, with its freezing winds, ice, and snow, the guanacos climb down the steep mountain

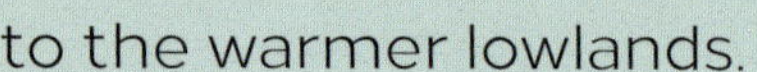

to the warmer lowlands.

At such great heights, winter temperatures will be below freezing for weeks. So in the fall, guanacos gather to begin their downward journey.

Summer sees guanacos in the hills and mountains, as high up as 13,000 feet. They feed on many plant foods, from soft flowers to tough twigs and prickly cacti.

Guanacos live in small herds of a leader male with several females and young, and separate males. A leader male kicks, butts, bites, and spits at rivals to keep them away.

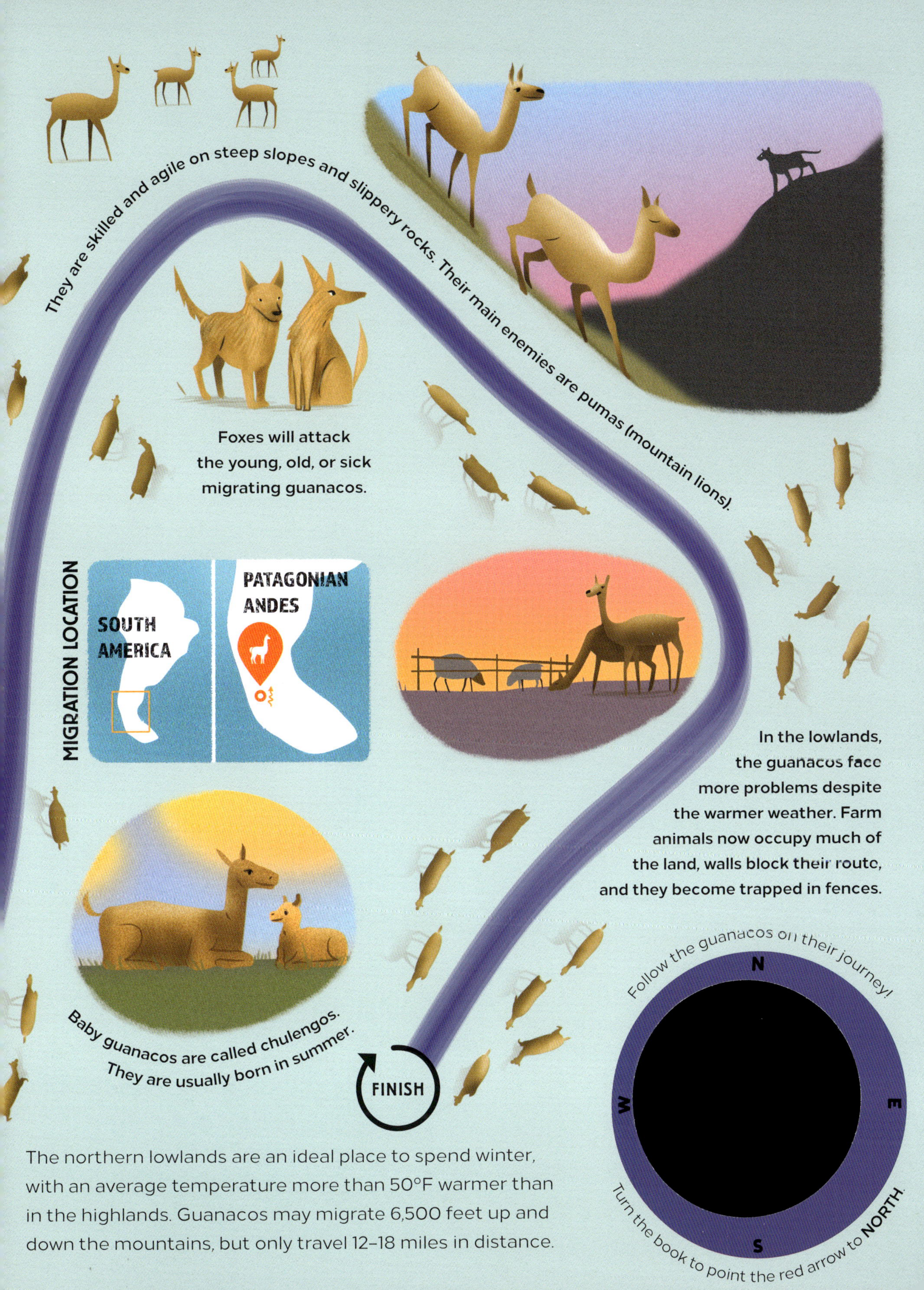

The northern lowlands are an ideal place to spend winter, with an average temperature more than 50°F warmer than in the highlands. Guanacos may migrate 6,500 feet up and down the mountains, but only travel 12–18 miles in distance.

PRAIRIE EXPEDITION

Pronghorns are the fastest land mammals in North America. They reach top speed when racing away from predators and sometimes when on migration, too. About one million pronghorns live on the prairies (grasslands) and open bushlands of America's midwest. Some stay in the same area all year. Others migrate, with herds heading north in spring for summer grazing and to raise their young, then south to avoid the northern winter. Their journeys, however, are becoming more difficult and deadly.

START

In the northern prairies, at the Grand Teton National Park in Wyoming, USA, early fall is pronghorn mating season. The arrival of cold winds and snow showers warn that winter is coming and it is time to leave.

The pronghorns gather into large herds of up to 400. Walking and trotting, they follow their regular migration trails southward.

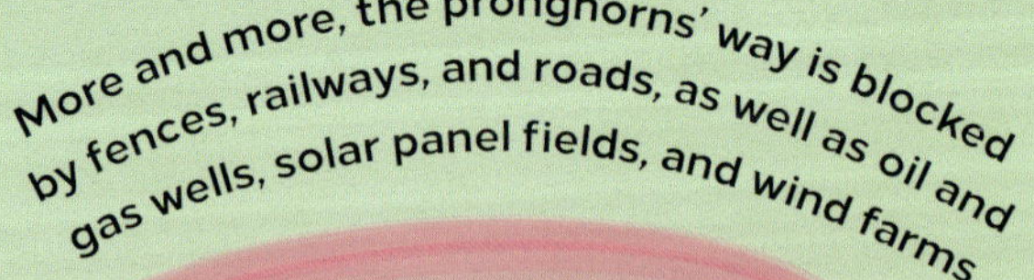

More and more, the pronghorns' way is blocked by fences, railways, and roads, as well as oil and gas wells, solar panel fields, and wind farms.

MIGRATION LOCATION

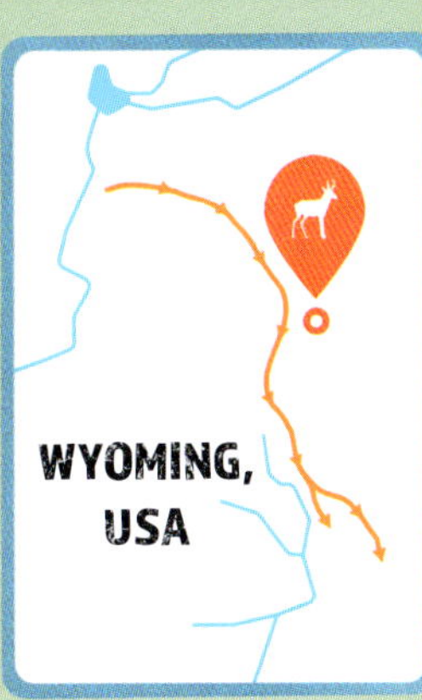

Predators, like mountain lions, wolves, eagles, and grizzly bears will prey on the pronghorns and their young along the journey.

Migration routes may pass through narrow, dangerous corridors, such as rocky gaps in the hills, or thin strips of countryside between towns.

After a journey of nearly 150 miles, the pronghorns reach their winter grazing areas. When spring comes, they will return north for summer. Their migration is one of the most difficult due to the many man-made obstacles along the way.

FINISH

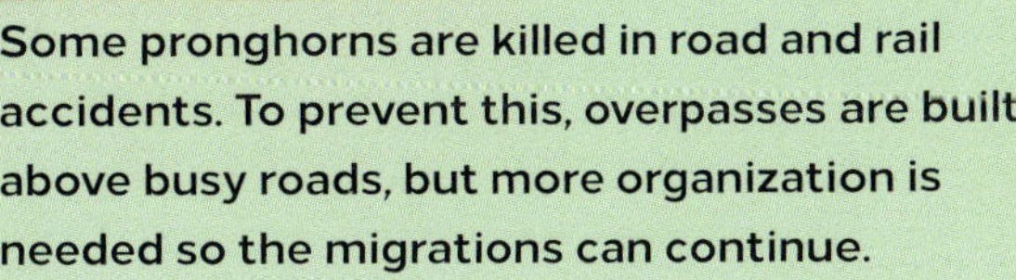

Some pronghorns are killed in road and rail accidents. To prevent this, overpasses are built above busy roads, but more organization is needed so the migrations can continue.

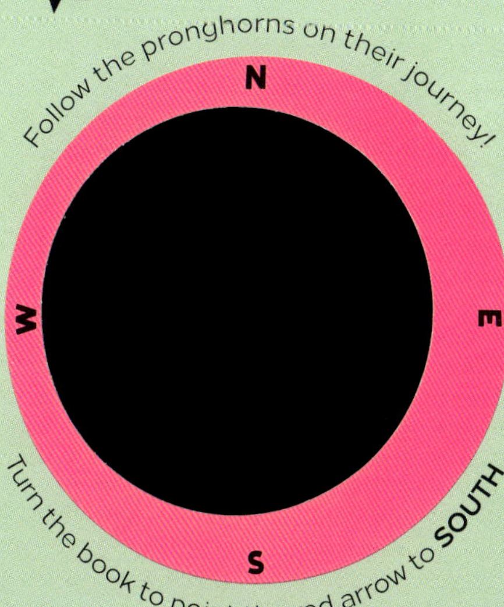

THE COLDEST MIGRATION

Emperors are the biggest penguins in the world and they number more than half a million. They live their whole lives in the ice-cold seas and on the ice-covered land of Antarctica. They migrate as part of their long-distance baby-care. Emperors raise their chicks on the ice, far inland from the sea. There are hardly any predators here. But it means there is a very long waddle between the breeding area, or rookery, and the open sea where they hunt for fish.

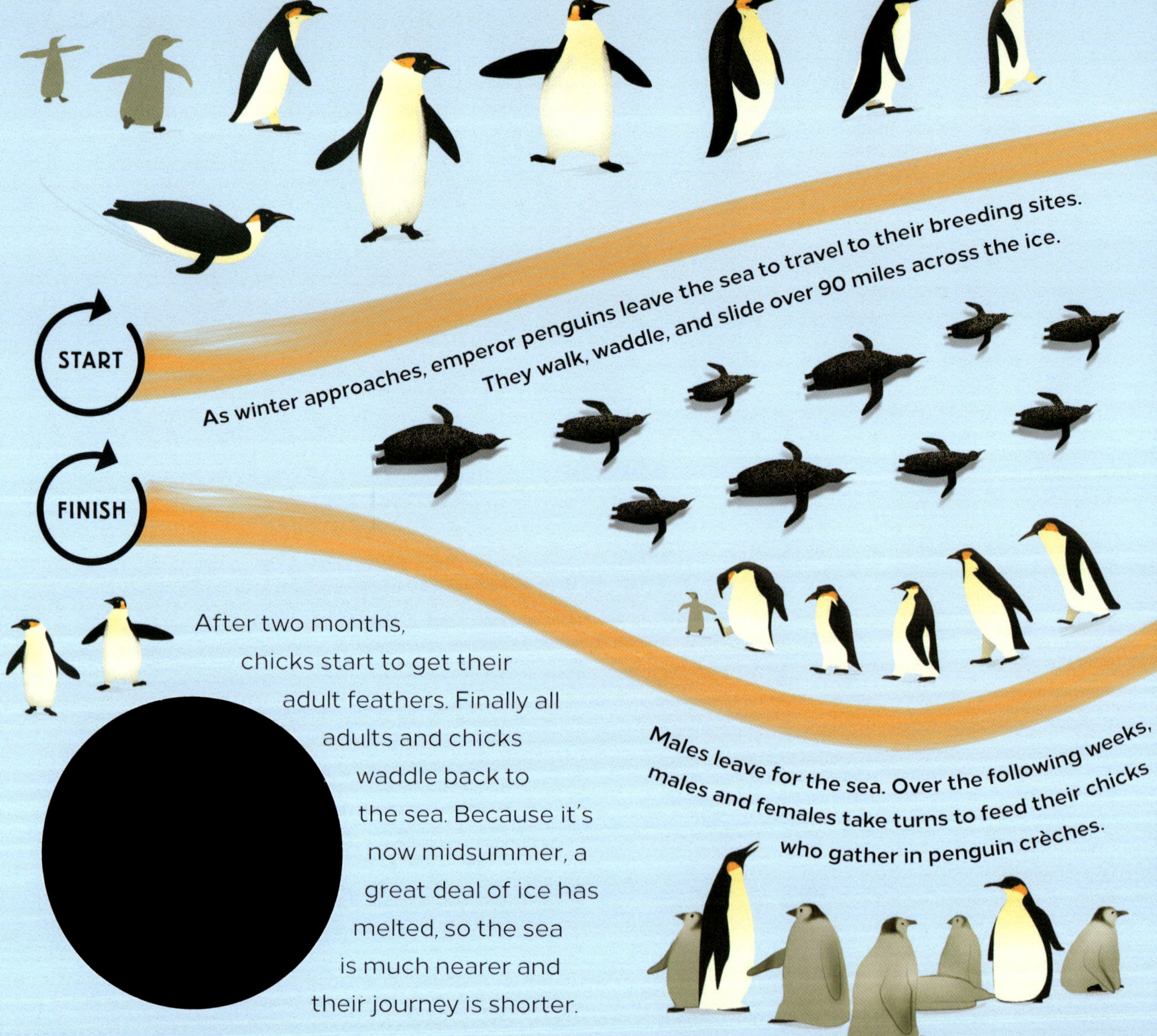

After two months, chicks start to get their adult feathers. Finally all adults and chicks waddle back to the sea. Because it's now midsummer, a great deal of ice has melted, so the sea is much nearer and their journey is shorter.

The female passes the egg to her partner's feet. He covers it with a special, warm skin fold, so it doesn't instantly freeze! It's -22°F!

At their regular rookery area, males and females pair up and mate. Several weeks later the female lays a single egg.

Females return to the sea to hunt for fish. For two months, males care for their eggs, huddling together for warmth to survive the blizzards during the coldest winter on Earth.

After the chick hatches, the male feeds it with coughed-up, or regurgitated, fish "soup."

Soon, well-fed females arrive from hunting fish in the sea. They cough up (regurgitate) more food to feed their young. The females will now take over from the males to care for their chicks.

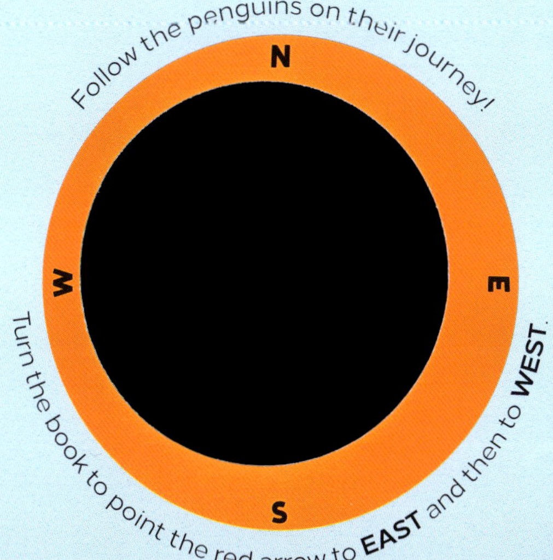

A CHRISTMAS JOURNEY

Most crabs live on the seashore or in the ocean. Christmas Island red crabs spend most of their lives in the forests on Christmas Island, in the Indian Ocean. They feed on the damp forest floor and hide from the sun in burrows. But as the rainy season begins, they start their journey to the coast—more than 20 million of them!

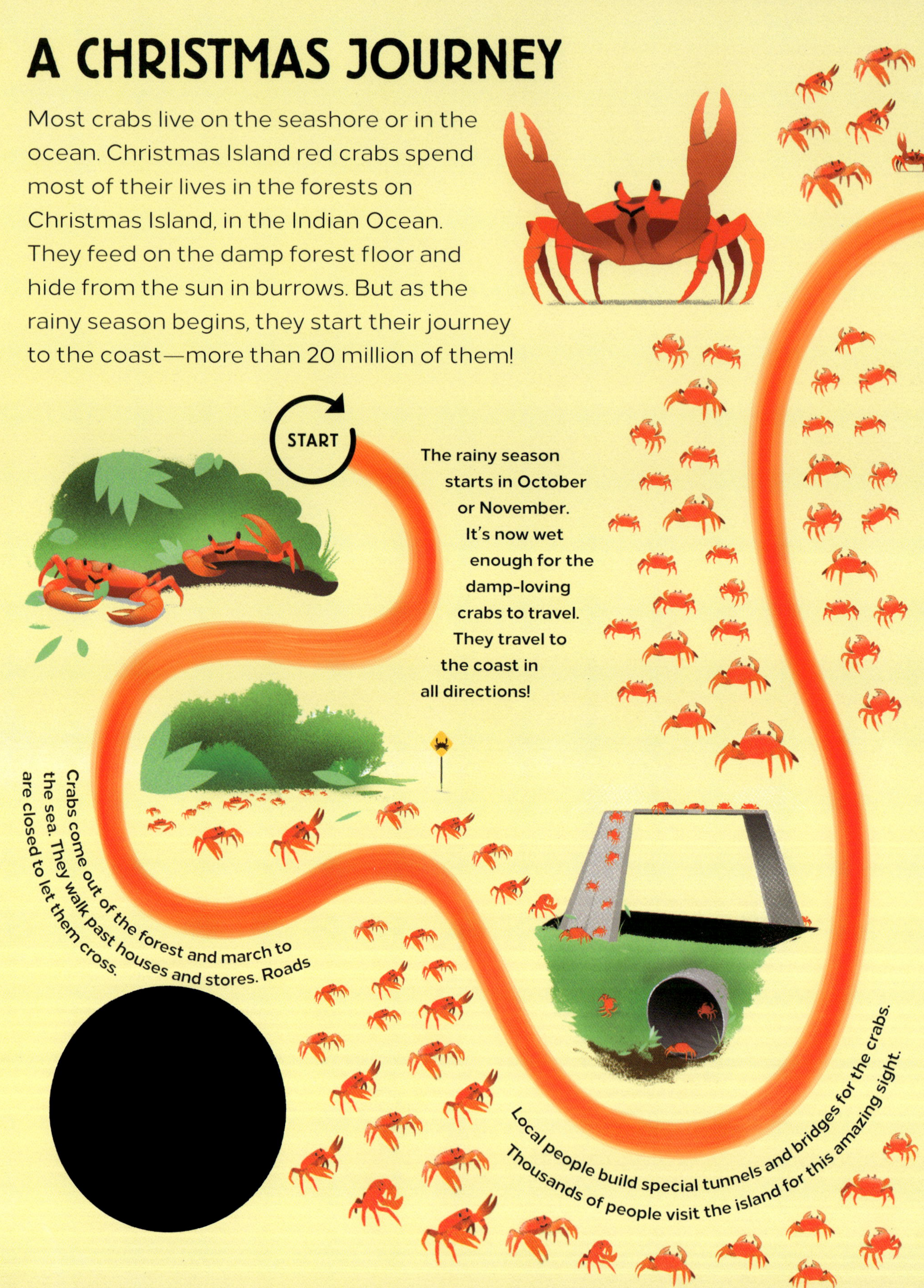

The rainy season starts in October or November. It's now wet enough for the damp-loving crabs to travel. They travel to the coast in all directions!

Crabs come out of the forest and march to the sea. They walk past houses and stores. Roads are closed to let them cross.

Local people build special tunnels and bridges for the crabs. Thousands of people visit the island for this amazing sight.